BORN WITH BIG FEET AND MADE TO MOVE

A Story About a Young Woman's Big Dream to Visit 25 Countries by the Age of 25 and What She Learned Along the Way.

Sara J. Gunn

AuthorHouse™
1663 Liberty Drive
Bloomington, IN 47403
www.authorhouse.com
Phone: 1 (800) 839-8640

Published by AuthorHouse: 12/14/2015

ISBN: 978-1-5049-2628-7 (sc)
ISBN: 978-1-5049-2630-0 (hc)
ISBN: 97-8-1504-92629-4 (e)

Print information available on the last page.

Any people depicted in stock imagery provided by Thinkstock are models,
and such images are being used for illustrative purposes only.
Certain stock imagery © Thinkstock.

This book is printed on acid-free paper.

authorHOUSE®

You were born with amazing feet. They are strong and can take you many places. Whether you have little feet, big feet, or you use wheels for feet, they are a gift.

So get out and see the world. You will find a suggested travel checklist of what to pack at the end of this book to help you take your trip from dream to action!

This is a story about a young woman named Sara. Sara had big feet, and the kids at school made fun of her and called her names. She was hurt by their words and thought something was wrong with her because she was different.

Yet Sara eventually found the true value of what made her different. Her courage and big feet allowed her to reach her big dream step-by-step. She visited many places, had many adventures, and made positive memories. In fact, she traveled to twenty-five countries by the time she was twenty-five years old.

Her feet took her on a bus from Dublin to the countryside in **Ireland**. She placed her feet in a pair of stirrups and went horseback riding across the lavish green hillside. It felt freeing to her to have the wind blowing her hair, hear the horses' hooves trot on the stone paths, smell a forest of pine trees on her right and see fields on her left.

She met nice, welcoming, and hospitable people in the beautiful country of **Ghana**. With her new friends, she tried to stay balanced as she wobbled on a canopy walkway in the treetops of Kakum National Park. Then, at Mole National Park, she encountered silly and entertaining baboons stealing fruit, soda, and ketchup bottles from the hotel pool and dining area. She even saw elephants, and their big feet, walking in their natural environment.

Traveling helped her learn more about herself and the world around her. She learned that she loves to study new cultures, try new things, and see all the different types of beautiful people, nature, and animals in the world. She fed birds, monkeys, and giraffes in **Thailand**. One giraffe got a kiss!

She tasted Belgian chocolate in **Belgium**. The Figaro truffle was silky, rich, and blended with hazelnut butter, milk chocolate, and dark chocolates.

Sara's feet danced while she listened to music by
the Vienna Philharmonic Orchestra in **Austria**.

Her feet allowed her to board a train to **Germany**.

As she walked in the forest, her feet crunched the colorful fallen autumn leaves. They were kissed by a light snowfall. Each leaf was different, and each one was beautiful!

With each step, she learned that her big feet were beautifully strong, useful, and supportive. Her big feet helped her move her body. They carried her up the vine-covered stairs of an ancient temple called Angkor Wat in **Cambodia**. She saw trees so old that they grew into and over the stones of the temple.

Her feet slid into a pair of ski boots so she could try skiing **Switzerland**'s big and beautiful snowy Alps in the sunshine and fresh air. Even though she felt the cold snow around her body after she slipped and fell, she stopped and saw the mountains from a different perspective. She felt a sense of peace and quiet. For a moment, it was just her and the view.

In the **Czech Republic**, She toured the streets and followed the sounds of live music as her feet took her across the beautiful Charles Bridge.

In **Poland**, her feet walked in the sacred footsteps of those who had walked before her in Auschwitz.

Your feet are a gift to be loved, even if they are big, small, or otherwise different.

Sara's feet took her to **Guatemala**, where she painted a mural of the country with volunteers.

She watched local entrepreneurs weave a blanket.

Then, with a tour guide leading the way, she hiked to the top of a volcano and roasted marshmallows off the heat of the hot lava!

She went kayaking on the canals of the **Netherlands**. She squeezed below low bridges and touched the underside of the cobblestone streets above her. She paddled next to houseboats on the edge of the canal, and she tried to dodge the water sprinkling toward her from nearby fountains.

Sara stepped into a river taxi that drifted away to a local farmers market on the Mekong River in **Laos**.

She learned that using her feet to travel the world brought her happiness. Material things did not bring her permanent happiness. For Sara, movement was the answer. Her big feet gave her the strength to move through many cities and countries and make happy memories with new people along the way.

She was even able to find this friend on the beach.

She saw interesting architecture throughout **Italy**, **France**, **Hungary**, **Luxembourg**, and **Slovakia**.

Sara traveled with the friends she met in Italy to a Legoland theme park in **Denmark**, where they walked through miniature worlds made of Legos and rode rollercoasters in the rain.

With her foot on the gas pedal, Sara drove from one side of **Slovenia** to the other and arrived in **Croatia**. She walked to the farmers market and bought fruits, vegetables, a basket and crafts made by local artisans.

She tried the local pizza and hot chocolate.

She also spotted an array of colors on the ground under her feet.

Later, she was able to experience the art and architecture of **Spain**, **England**, **Scotland**, and **Malaysia**. She used her feet to explore. She discovered the beauty of diversity. Different is beautiful whether it is in how you look, your hair, ears, height, legs, or in the world's diverse landscapes, foods, languages, people, music, dance, paintings, and more. Travel helped Sara learn to accept the beauty in things that are different, including her big feet!

Happiness can exist only in acceptance.

—- George Orwell. English novelist and journalist

Finally, hand-in-hand with her twin sister, Sara used her big feet to hike the trails and sand dunes of Michigan in the **United States**.

She made many friends along the path to her big dream—and you will too! You just have to move.

People travel for many reasons. People travel to relax. They travel to try something new. They travel to visit friends and family. They also travel to volunteer to build homes or give back to their communities by helping others.

She met many people around the world who were all different, but she discovered that they had the same wants and needs, to be safe and happy no matter where or how they were born.

Even though she was scared at first to try new things and be so far away from her home, family, and friends, she found that traveling was exciting and rewarding. She explored twenty-five countries and saw many different beaches, mountains, trees, animals and flowers. She experienced unique foods, sights, smells, and sounds. She discovered that it is great to stretch her limits, make new memories, and try something completely different than what she once knew.

This was all thanks to her big feet!

Love yourself first, and everything else falls into line.

—Lucille Ball, American actress and comedian

She loves herself, including her strong feet. They have given her many gifts, helped her move, and brought lasting happiness!

1. Dublin, Ireland, Europe
2. Tema, Ghana, West Africa
3. Hua-Hin, Thailand, Asia
4. Brussels, Belgium, Europe
5. Vienna, Austria, Europe

6. Kaiserslautern, Germany, Europe
7. Siem Reap, Cambodia, Asia
8. Geneva, Switzerland, Europe
9. Prague, Czech Republic, Europe
10. Auschwitz, Poland, Europe

11. Antigua, Guat
Central America
12. Leiden, the N
13. Mekong Rive
14. Rome, Italy, E
15. Paris, France,

ARCTIC OCEAN

Sample Packing List and Tips for Parents

When traveling internationally, don't forget to pack these suggested items:

☐ Passport and visa

Tip: Check online to see if you'll need to apply for a visa for the country you're visiting. Check the expiration date on your passport to ensure it will not expire while you are abroad. The expiration date should also be more than 90 days from your last day of travel. Keep a copy of the photo page and visa page of your passport in case it gets lost.

☐ Plane ticket and travel itinerary

☐ Driver's license or other ID card

Tip: To earn special discounts on some museums, activities, accommodations, and food, full-time students can get an International Student Identity Card (ISIC), people between the ages of twelve and thirty years old who are not full-time students can get an International Youth Travel Card (IYTC), and full-time teachers or professors can get an International Teacher Identity Card (ITIC). Ordering your card online takes three to four weeks for delivery, depending on the postal system in your country.

☐ Camera and camera charger

☐ Language translation book, guide, or app, in case you are going to a place where you don't know the language.

Tip: Learning a few words and phrases in the local language can make all the difference in earning respect from locals.

☐ Luggage tags

Tip: Tie a colored ribbon or add duct tape onto your checked bag so you can easily identify it in baggage claim after the flight (a lot of luggage looks the same). Also, take a photo of your luggage and/or add your name and phone number to the outside of your bags in case they get lost.

☐ Snacks (that won't spill or melt in your bag), games, music and entertainment for the flight

☐ Cash and coins in the country's local currency

Tip: You may need this before you get to the Currency Exchange Center at your destination's airport. In European countries it is helpful to have coins handy because it sometimes costs 50 cents to use the public toilet (i.e. the WC or "water closet").

☐ Address(es) and phone number(s) of your accommodations. Also consider giving a copy to a friend or family member back home in case they need to reach you.

☐ Map of the areas you intend to visit

☐ Transportation schedule

☐ Adapters and converters if your destination's electrical outlets/sockets are not the same shape as the plugs on your appliances.

☐ Your supply of medicines

☐ Clothes that do not wrinkle easily and ones that you can layer or remove depending on weather changes.

Tip: Bring a plastic bag to put your dirty clothes in after you wear them.

☐ Hygiene products: toothbrush, toothpaste, hairbrush, hand wipes, travel size tissues, etc.

☐ Sunglasses and/or hat

☐ A journal or device to document your new memories

☐ Pictures from home to show your new friends

☐ Your happy heart and beautiful smile

☐ Finally, comfortable walking shoes to ensure you take care of your feet!

Safe travels!

My wish is that you make great memories, learn great lessons, and have fun as you explore!

You are different and unique and that is amazing ... just as our world is a diverse, beautiful, and amazing place!

Printed in the United States
by Baker & Taylor Publisher Services